THE MIST
OF
MY HEART
Selected Poems of Shu Ting

Translated by
Gordon T. Osing & De-an Wu Swihart

Edited by William O'Donnell

Panda Books

Panda Books
First Edition 1995
Copyright © CHINESE LITERATURE PRESS 1995
ISBN 7−5071−0285−8
ISBN 0−8351−3148−3

Published by CHINESE LITERATURE PRESS
Beijing 100037, China
Distributed by China International Book Trading Corporation
35 Chegongzhuang Xilu, Beijing 100044, China
P.O. Box 399, Beijing, China
Printed in the People's Republic of China

CONTENTS

Introduction   5

Editorial Note   18

Autobiographical Note by Shu Ting   21

Poems   25

  From *A Boat with Two Masts* (1982)   27
    Morning Song at the Seashore   27
    Ah, Mama   29
    Seeing a Friend Off on an Autumn Evening   30
    For You   31
    On Mid-Autumn Moon Festival   32
    Wishes   33
    Self-portrait   34
    The Cypress Vine Dreams of the Moon   36
    April Dusk   37
    This Is Also "All"   38
    Motherland, My Dear Motherland   40
    The Cry of a Generation   41
    To My Generation   43
    After the Storm Is Over   44
    A Love Poem to the Land   47
    On Your Going-away: A Gift   49
    Untitled   50

  From *Selected Lyrics of Shu Ting and Gu Cheng* (1982)   51
    To a Poet of Fairy Tales   51
    ? . !   52

At Dusk	54
On the Painting "A Young Lady at the Spring"	55
Returning in Dream	56
To the Legendary Lady of Huian	57
At a Dank Little Station	58
The Wall	59
A White Swan	60
From *The Singing Iris* (1986)	61
The Heart Has Its Own Law	61
"I Love You"	63
Words for a Stele	64
An Old House	65
To a Friend Going Abroad	66
Goddess Peak	67
A Poem I Wish I Had Read to My Mother	68
A Monument for My Mother	69
Fled to the Moon	70
White Palms	71
In Memory of Grandmother	72
From *Archaeopteryx* (1992)	73
A Concert at St. Mary's	73
Forget-me-nots	74
Where Zen is Cultivated	75
Shui Xian	76
A Room with Two Beds	78
Guanyin, Drop by Drop	81
Prose	85
People, Please Understand Me (1980)	85
Essays	87
Life, Books, and Poetry (1980)	89
Complete Silence from the Clarity Gained through Sadness (1984)	102

Introduction

BEIJING University's distinguished poetry critic Xie Mian, an influential supporter of Misty Poetry, has vividly described Shu Ting in his book On Modern Chinese Poets: "When she wrote poems in an unconventional way, a storm of condemnation struck her. Her ways of thinking and feeling were regarded as heresy.... But she had already started her journey, she had no other choice but to be crucified on the cross of poetry."* At the start of the 1980s Shu Ting was recognized as a rising star in Chinese poetry and a representative poet of the generation that had grown up during the "cultural revolution" (1966-76). But at the same time he was criticized for her departures from the conventional style of writing. Some readers thought her allusive poetic imagery was obscure or "misty," and her poetry exhibits a distinctly personal and female perspective that was new to modern Chinese literary history. No other woman poet had captured such national attention in China in the twentieth century.

Born in Shima, near Zhangzhou, Fujian in 1952, Shu Ting grew up in a broken family. When she was five years old, her father was denounced in the Anti-Rightist Campaign and was sent to a mountain village. Her mother divorced him to reduce the effects of his political troubles on their three children. Then she and the children moved to Xiamen, the capital city of Fujian. Those were difficult times. Shu Ting lived with her mother and grandmother, but was separated both from her old brother, who had been sent to live with his paternal grandmother,

---

*Xie Mian, *On Modern Chinese Poets* (Zhongguo Xiandai Shiren Lun), Chongqing Press, 1986.

and from her younger sister, who had been sent to live with an aunt. Shu Ting's mother felt miserable about the family situation, and although during the day she was a firm, hard-working mother, at night she cried secretly with a broken heart. Shu Ting acknowledges, in her autobiographical essays that are included in this book, that her mother's combination of rich depths of feeling and a weak disposition had a great impact on her own personality, which is reflected in her poetry. Her mother's difficult situation aroused Shu Ting's concern about women's problems. Many of her poems and essays are about women — mother, grandmother, girls, female friends, widows, and even a legendary goddess. Shu Ting's grandmother, who was a Christian, became an important influence on her. Shu Ting recalls in her essay "Inspirations from Gods" (1986): "Every night before going to bed, she knelt before a window and prayed to God, while a peaceful and sublime light appeared on her face. To be with god was the only wish in her heart."* Perhaps to some extent, Christianity's emphasis on love is reflected in the attention Shu Ting pays to love. Romantic love has long been a familiar theme in Western poetry, but was not then a feature of conventional Chinese poetry. Shu Ting's love poems immediately became popular with readers who, after enduring the excesses of the "cultural revolution," now thirsted for love, trust, and honesty.

The "cultural revolution" had seriously disrupted Shu Ting's education after the eighth grade, and in 1969, at age seventeen, she was sent to a mountain village in west Fujian. She continued her self-education by learning characters from a dictionary and by reading. In 1970 she started writing poems, often to enclose in letters to her friends. Many of those early poems reflect the particular occasion of their composition, such as "Seeing a Friend Off on an Autumn Evening" (1975). In 1972, after

---

The Mist of My Heart (Xinyan), Shanghai Literature and Art Press, 1988, pp 176−177.

three years in the countryside, she returned to Xiamen, only to spend the next several years unemployed or holding only temporary jobs. Her feeling of estrangement from a world that failed to accept her is powerfully evident in poems such as "Morning Song at the Seashore" (1975) and "Sailboat" (1975), which opens:

> A small boat is,
> for whatever reasons,
> stranded sideways
> on a desolate, rocky shore,*

Her unemployment did provide her time to observe life, to think, and to write many poems. Her poems, still unpublished, were widely circulated hand to hand among youths in Fujian and became very popular. This brought her many friends who shared her interest in poetry, the most important of whom was Cai Qijiao, an older poet who had been sent to a mountain area of Fujian for "reform through labor." He became her mentor and had a great influence on her writing through his many long letters about poetry technique and theory, sometimes referring to an anthology of Western literary theory (Xifang wenlun xuan), from Plato to the twentieth century, published in 1964. In 1977 Cai Qijiao sent her some poems written by innovative young Beijing poets. In her essay "Life, Books, and Poetry" she has recorded how their poetry had a powerful effect on her writing. In December 1978, Shu Ting's poems "Ah, Mama" (1975) and "To the Oak Tree" (1977) were published in the first issue of the magazine *Today (Jintian)*, in Beijing. An editor of *Today* wrote to tell her that when the issue was displayed in Beijing more readers wrote admiring comments under her two poems than any others in the magazine. She became a frequent contributor to that magazine. In October 1979, Shu Ting vis-

---

*"Saliboat" (1975), *A Boat with Two Masts* (Shuangkui Chuan), Shanghai Literature and Art Press, 1982, p. 12.

ited Beijing, where she met *Today*'s group for a poetry reading. That same year, *Poetry Journal (Shikan)*, a prestigious national monthly magazine, printed her "To the Oak Tree" and then several more of her poems. Here is the poem "To the Oak Tree" that made her immediately famous and one of the brightest rising stars in poetry circles:

To the Oak Tree

If I really love you —
I won't climb over you like the trumpet-creeper
standing on your highest branch to show.
If I really love you —
I won't imitate the infatuated bird,
calling endlessly to your green shade;
I will not be merely the available spring
that comforts you with cool waters year around,
nor merely a dramatic precipice, either,
that sets off your grandeur, or heightens your dignities,
nor even your sunlight,
nor your spring rains.
No, all of these are not enough to be me!
I must be another, a kapok tree, near you,
definitely another tree standing there with you,
our roots entwined in the earth,
our leaves brushing each other in the mists.
Each time when a breeze sways us,
we give our regards to each other
but no one else
needs to understand us.
You have your bronze reaches and iron girth,
like broadswords and sabers,
like spears;
I have my red flowers,
large as heavy sighs,

bright as torches.
We share the cold waves, the wind, the thunderstorms, and
   the lightning;
we share the mists, the fog, and the rainbows.
It might seem we grow apart always
but we will depend on each other all our lives.
This only can be a real love,
true fidelity in
love —
not only for your magnificence,
but also for the position your hold firmly, and for the land
   holding you.*

Also in 1979, the magazine Orchid Garden (Lanhua pu), in Fuzhou, Fujian, published a group of her poems, which drew so much attention that the respected provincial magazine, Fujian Literature (Fujian wenxue), for eleven monthly issues starting in February 1980 had a special section exclusively for debate about her poetry. This was one important event in what became a decade-long, nationwide debate over "Misty Poetry."

The Misty Poetry emerged in the late 1970s with the sudden prominence of several young poets like Shu Ting. Their poetry styles were very unconventional but also very unlike the directness of style used by New Realism prose fiction after the "cultural revolution" ended in 1976. In the debate in literary circles across China over Misty Poetry's obscure content and modernist techniques for poetic expression, both sides regarded Shu Ting as the single most representative Misty poet. In addition to the eleven special sections in Fujian Literature in 1980, a leading literary critical journal, Modern Trend of Literary Thinking (Dangdai wenyi sichao) held a discussion of her poetry in 1985, and dozens of other articles about her poetry were published in magazines across China during the debate. As we will

---

*Poetry Journal (Shikan), 1979, No. 4; collected in A Boat with Two Masts, pp. 16−17.

see, Shu Ting's election to the Board of Directors of the Chinese Writers' Association in 1984 was an important indication of the new-found national acceptance of Misty Poetry.

Between 1979 and 1981 she published more than one hundred poems in magazines throughout China. She won a national award in 1980 for her poem "Motherland, My Dear Motherland" (1979). In 1982 Shanghai Literary Press published her first book of poems, *A Boat with Two Masts (Shuangkui Chuan)*, containing forty-seven poems written from 1971 to 1981. That book was awarded a prize as the best new collection of poetry. The year 1981 also saw publication of a joint collection with Gu Cheng, *Selected Lyrics of Shu Ting and Gu Cheng (Shu Ting, Gu Cheng Shuqingshi Xuan)*, published by Fujian People's Press.

In the Winter of 1981, Shu Ting's sixteen-section poem "The Singing Iris" appeared and drew a storm of unexpectedly harsh criticism, some of which even impugned her personally, without cause. This, on top of the continuing heated controversy over her other poems, caused her much suffering, as she poignantly recounts in her essay "Complete Silence from the Clarity Gained Through Sadness." She chose the dignity of silence as her resistance to the unfair criticism, as she explains in that essay, and as is reflected in her poem "The Heart Has Its Own Law" (1976). She kept silent until the Spring of 1984, when she started again to publish poems. At the end of that year she was elected to the Board of Directors of the Chinese Writers' Association.

But during even those three years of her silence the changes in Chinese poetry that she had helped initiate continued to evolve rapidly. A newer generation of poets, mostly college students, was rising to prominence all across China. They organized their own poetry clubs and published their own magazines that concentrated on a wide range of very active experimentation in poetry writing. These "Third Generation" poets openly called for artistic expression that would move beyond the Misty Poetry, of which Shu Ting stands as an exemplar. In 1986, the same year that Shu Ting published her third book of poems, The Singing Iris, eighty-four Third Generation poetry groups attending a national conference in Shenzhen, Guangdong, asserted that they had already passed beyond the era of Misty Poetry.

It was true that by 1986 the publication of each new poem by Shu Ting no longer created almost sensational excitement, as had earlier been the case. But her 1986 collection, The Singing Iris, shows an increasingly refined artistry that has continued to develop in her 1992 collection, which takes its title from an 1985 poem about an extinct pre-historic bird with reptile-like teeth and bony tail, *Archaeopteryx* (pronounced "ar-key-op-tah-riks").

The essays by Shu Ting in this book remind us that prose writing has been an increasingly important part of her career since 1986. She collected forty essays, written between 1972 and 1987, in *The Mist of My Heart*, published by Shanghai Literature and Art Press in 1988. That has been recently followed by a second collection of essays, *Carefree Life* (Fujian: Lujian Press, 1994). Most of the early essays focus on her memories of childhood or her life when she was in the countryside. Her later prose writings are like skillfully expressive paintings that take a detail from life and place it in a broad setting to express her particular thinking about life.

Shu Ting married a poetry critic and college teacher, Chen Zhongyi, in 1982. They both had grown up on Gulangyu, a small island near Shamen, where they now live with their young son. Her essays underscore the importance that she places on being a poet, wife, and mother. Shu Ting is the most popular Chinese woman poet of the twentieth century. The poem that first established her fame, "To the Oak Tree", expresses a woman's determination to be equal with a man. In a recent interview Shu Ting said that this poem, which is widely admired, is a declaration of equality, independence, and freedom for women in China and for all humanity.* Before that poem it was difficult to find any Chinese feminist poetry. The conventional writing in China usually silenced the specific voice of women by elevating the working class — female and male alike — above the individual. Rather than female or male characters there are members of a party or class, without regard to gender. Many of Shu Ting's poems reveal the awakening of a feminist consciousness. For instance, "To the Legendary Lady of Huian" describes the suffering a widow endures and absence of enjoyment in her life as she fulfills the Confucian dictate to remain chaste and faithful to her dead husband's memory. "Goddess Peak" (1981) further expresses a woman's voice of rebellion against the old ways of a woman's life, by calling, in a woman's voice, to

> ... spread a new rebellion:
> Better to cry away one night on a lover's shoulder
> than be the stone star on a famous cliff a thousand years.

A recent poem "A Room with Two Beds" (1988) ironically portrays the poet's friendship with another female poet. The twin beds are a metaphor for their sister-like close relation as woman writers, each of whom is at the same time a wife and mother. Both are fond of Virginia Woolf's idea of "A Room of One's Own," but the poem makes clear how far short the condition of Chinese women writers falls of that expectation. The ideas and the expression of Shu Ting's poems usually have a distinctively feminist quality and language that places her as an important woman writer in modern China.

Another distinctive mark of Shu Ting's poems is the presence of an emotional and intensely personal response to the objective world. This subjectivity or "self-expression" (biaoxian ziwo), as it was often called during the Misty Poetry debates, is a major innovation in her poems. She often uses an "I" speaker to convey feelings shared by her generation — loneliness, sad-

---

* Personal interview with Shu Ting, July 15, 1994.

ness, disspiritedness, and despair. Her "Motherland, My Dear Motherland" (1979) is an important early example of that method. In that poem, the "I" speaks of herself as she is the history and social condition of her motherland:

> I am that old water-wheel in ruins on the river's bank,
> that for hundreds of years past spun a weary song:
> I am the blackened miner's lamp on your forehead,
> lighting not quite the tunnel where you grope for history.
> I am the dried, empty spikes of rice in the field, the potholed road,
> the barge on a silted shoal,
> the two-ropes
>   cutting into your shoulder.
> — O motherland!
>
> I the poverty,
> I the sorrow
> I have been for generations
>   the bitter pain of your hope;

The "I" speaker in that poem interchanges her identity with her motherland. The "I" speaks as if she is the history and social conditions of the motherland, while the "I" is also a marrating personal consciousness that expresses an individual's beliefs.

Most of Shu Ting's poems have images that provide multiple suggestions of meaning that reflect the psychosocial dissonances of the world in which she lives. A famous example is in the opening lines of her poem "Sailboat", the boat that has run aground becomes a metaphor of her own situation of being stranded in life. The poem says that the boat is only a few meters away from the sea, but in that short distance the sea has lost all its immense power. That image reveals a general disappointment at being unable to achieve goals in life, even though they might seem to be within what ought to be easy reach. In her poem "At a Dank Little Station" (1977), the image of a girl waiting fruitlessly on the railroad station platform can expand to the universal resonance of Samuel Beckett's *Waiting for Godot*. The dead leaf in Shu Ting's "Fallen Leaf" is a powerful metaphor or spiritual death, in the poem's final stanza, as the first-person speaker metamorphoses into a leaf. That confusion of identity suggests the instability of the speaker's world:

> Suddenly I feel I am a fallen leaf, too,
> lying on the dark earth.
> The wind might be a dirge for me.
> I wait peacefully
> for the green dream
> to gleam once again in my body.*

Shu Ting is willing to present intense images and not provide explicit connections between them. For instance, her "Two, Maybe Three Different Memories" juxtaposes seven images in its first eight lines without direct links. Is this the poet's stream of consciousness, remembered fragments from a sexual encounter, or description of drunkenness? The reader is left to choose among the possibilities:

> The wine cup turned over,
> a stone path floats beneath the moonlight;
> where grasses were beaten down
> an azalea has been dropped and abandoned.
>
> Eucalyptus trees begin to spin,
> stars turning together — a kaleidoscope;
> on a rusted iron anchor,
> the dizzy sky is caught in my eyes.**

---

* "Fallen Leaf" (publ. 1980), *A Boat with Two Masts*, p. 25.
** "Two, Maybe Three Different Memories" (May 23, 1978), *A Boat with Two Masts*, p. 48.

Shu Ting's poetry often juxtaposes opposing images, even within a single line, as occurs in each of these lines from Shu Ting's "Wishes" (1976):

> Nights are hidden in your shadow, like the grave,
>   but also like the cradle.
> The winds conceal your footprints, like funeral music,
>   but are also a bugle sounding

In the first of those lines, the pairing of "grave" and "cradle" suggest the dual aspects of night, as darkness like death and as that from which a new day is born.

Although most of Shu Ting's poems retain the freedom to vary the lengths of each line and stanza, she suggests patterns and creates a musical result by placing rhyme words at the end of every two or four lines in a stanza, but allowing the rhyme to change from stanza to stanza. She also introduces flexibly some of the formal elements of classical poetry, such as repetition and parallelism. One of the several instances of repetition is in "Wishes" (1976) where each of the first twelve lines begins with "I wish." Classical poems often use elaborate parallelism between two lines. That can be found in many of Shu Ting's poems, for example these two lines from "To a Poet of Folktales" (1980), given here in Pinyin and in a verbatim English rendering:

> *xin yexu hen xiao hen xiao,*
> *shijie que hen da hen da.*

> heart perhaps [is] very small very small,
> world however [is] very large very large.

She often varies that technique by placing the parallel lines in separate stanzas.

Shu Ting's technical skill enriches her poetic voice that speaks so fluently, sincerely, and perceptively of this remarkable woman and her world. In 1986 the International Conference on Modern Chinese Literature was convened in Shanghai, with invitations to many foreign experts on Chinese Literature, but to only a few Chinese writers, each of whom represented a literary genre. Shu Ting received the invitation for poetry, and her talk at that conference helped to make her known internationally. Since then she has made nine trips abroad, with visits to France, Germany, Holland, Italy, the United States, and five other countries. Her poems have been translated into more than twenty languages, and four book-length collections have been published in Austria, Denmark, France, and Germany. We hope that this book will bring Shu Ting to many new readers.

In 1990, with Gordon Osing and William O'Donnell, I started translating the first Anthology of Misty Poetry (Menglong shixuan), published in China in 1982. That influential anthology opens with thirty-one poems by Shu Ting, far more than any of the other eleven poets in that book. While we were translating her poems I corresponded with her, and she kindly send me all of her poetry collections and autobiographical essays, and her husband's literary articles on poetry. In our continuing correspondence she has provided much information about her career as a writer and about individual poems. After we finished translating the Anthology of Misty Poetry we decided, with the encouragement of the Chinese Literature Press, to translate a comprehensive collection of Shu Ting's poems, reflecting the path of her continuing creative development. Her autobiographical essays provide background and personal insights for the poems. In the Summer of 1994 I visited Shu Ting and her family in Xiamen, Fujian. Those three days at her very pleasant house on Gulangyu Island were filled with long talks that gave me a keen appreciation of her personality, her thinking, and her life in the lovely environment where she has created many of her poems.

We believe that the first concern of the translations should be to communicate the artistic merit of the poems to readers of the English versions. I prepared preliminary English versions and then worked with poet Gordon Osing as he improved them as poems in English. The resulting translations reflect Professor Osing's skill and creativity as a poet, although I retain responsibility for their linguistic accuracy. William O'Donnell assisted me with the prose sections of the book and then edited the full manuscript.

De-an Wu Swihart

Editorial Note

THE poems in this book, selected from Shu Ting's four major collections, are arranged chronologically, except for *Selected Lyrics of Shu Ting and Gu Cheng (Shu Ting, Gu Cheng Shuqingshi Xuan,* Fujian People's Press, 1982). That joint collection emphasized the parallels between the two poets by intermixing their poems, without any identification of the author or date of each poem. That volume begins with two dedicatory poems, one by each poet, and then has four thematic sections. The selections here are given in the order used in that volume. Shu Ting's dedicatory poem to Gu Cheng, "To a Poet of Folk-tales," was reprinted from her first collection, earlier that same year, *A Boat with Two Masts (Shuangkui Chuan,* Shanghai Literature and Art Press, 1982). The four sections and the poems selected from them are: I. Hanging Green Apple, II. Harbor of the Heart ("?.!" and "At Dusk"), III. Toward the Dense Forest of the World ("On the Painting Young Lady at the Spring" and "Returning in Dream"), and IV. Song of Seven Colors ("To the Legendary Lady of Huian" through "A White Swan — Killed in Beijing"). The four poems marked with an asterisk were reprinted in the third collection, *The Singing Iris (Hui Changge de Yuanweihua,* Sichuan Literature and Art Press, 1986). Her fourth and most recent collection is *Archaeopteryx* (Shizuniao, Haixia Literature and Art Press, 1992). We have provided a few explanatory footnotes to assist the reader.

Shu Ting has revised her "Autobiographical Note" for this book. Her brief essay "People, Please Understand Me" was first published, untitled, in *Poetry Journal (Shikan, Beijing)*, 1980, No. 10; it is printed here with the title that was added in 1982 by the editors Yan Yuejun, Liang Yun, Gao Yan, and Gu Fang of the *Anthology of Misty Poetry (Menglong shixuan)*, which was internally published by the Liaoning University Chinese Department, Literary Research Center.

Gordon T. Osing and De-an Wu Swihart, who are colleagues of mine at the University of Memphis, and I hope that our complementary expertise in poetry writing, in Chinese literature and language, in modern British and American poetry, and in editing, has enabled us to produce a useful selection of Shu Ting's poetry and autobiographical prose, all rendered in English that is accurate, while aspiring to be lively and poignant as the Chinese originals. Throughout the preparation of this book Shu Ting has generously provided information that has helped us in preparing the translations and the notes.

Poet Gordon T. Osing, who recently taught for three years in China and Hong *Kong, has co-translated* Chinese poetry in three recent books: *City at the End of Time* (includes 40 poems by Hong Kong's Leung Ping-Kwan; Hong Kong University Culture Studies series, 1992; five co-translations with Leung Ping-Kwan will be published in Renditions); *Forever Tonight at My Window: Thirty Ci of Li Qing Zhao (1992)* and *Blooming Alone in Winter: Fifty Poems by Su Tung P'o* (1990; both with Min Xiao-Hong and Huang Hai-Peng; Zhengzhou: Henan People's Publishing House). He has published two collections of his own poems, T*own Down-river* (1985) and *From the Boundary Waters* (1981) and 70 poems in national journals including The New Yorker, The Southern Review, Kansas Quarterly, Hawaii Pacific Review, and Poetry Northwest.

Chinese literature scholar De-an Wu Swihart is a native of Beijing and a member of Shu Ting's generation which had the "cultural revolution" interrupt their schooling. Then as a writer and student of Chinese Literature at Beijing University from 1978-1982, she knew several of the Misty poets and read some of their poems before publication. Since 1982 she has lived in the United States, earning an M.A. at the University of Chicago and a Ph.D. (East Asian Studies) at Princeton University in 1990. She teaches Chinese language and literature.

I, a modern poetry scholar and editor, assisted De-an Wu Swihart with the prose translation and edited the full manuscript. I have written two books on W. B. Yeats and is editor of three volumes in the new collected edition of Yeats and one volume in the Cornell University Press series of manuscript transcriptions.

Publication of this book, and travel by De-An Wu Swihart, have been supported by the University of Memphis and its College of Arts and Sciences, the Department of English, and Department of Foreign Languages and Literatures.

William H. O'Donnell

Autobiographical Note by Shu Ting

1952: On April 25th I was born in Shima, near Zhangzhou, Fujian. I was called Gong Peiyu until I entered elementary school, at age six, when I became Gong Shuting.
1957: My father was sent to a village in a mountainous region of Fujian for "reform through labor" after he was denounced as a rightist during the Anti-Rightist Campaign. My mother divorced him, and I was raised by my maternal grandmother in Xiamen. Even as a child I often did not conform to the normal way of life and was criticized for "petite bourgeois sentiments."
1964: At the First Middle School in Xiamen I was more interested in biology than literature. When the "cultural revolution" began, a year and a half later, I first fancifully joined in, but after a half year I turned to the "carefree school" — hiding at home and reading Balzac, Hugo, and Tolstoy.
1969: I was sent to live and work in the Taiba People's Commune in western Fujian. During those years [among the mostly illiterate mountain villagers] my intellectual life consisted of writing a diary and letters to my friends, and hurriedly reading the secretly circulated copies of literary masterpieces. I also wrote some short poems that eventually began to circulate among the youths who had been sent to the countryside. When I left the mountain village, after three years, I burned most of my diary and my other writings except for a few poems.
1972: I returned to Xiamen, and in the next eight years I was as-

signed temporary jobs in factories as a bricklayer, textile mile worker, solderer in a light bulb factory, and statistician. Because I insisted that I did not want an administrative office job I tasted all the hardships of front-line workers.

1974: After being introduced by a friend, I began to correspond with the older poet Cai Qijiao, who had been sent to do manual labor in Yongan, Fujian. He was very supportive of my poetry writing. I was impressed by his eagerness to explore new things. Later he introduced me to some young poets and I joined their circles, and published my poems "To the Oak Tree" and "Ah, Mama" in a mimeographed magazine in 1978.

1979: In April, *Poetry Journal* reprinted "To the Oak Tree," which was my first poem to be published in an official magazine. Several of my poems were also published in another mimeographed magazine, *Orchid Garden*, in 1979. Those poems ignited a stormy debate.

1980: The publisher of *Poetry Journal* sponsored the first Youth Poetry Conference and invited me to Beijing to attend. At the end of that year I was transferred to a job at the Fujian Federation of Writers and Artists. Fujian Literature, in its February 1980 issue, began a special section titled "On Shu Ting's Poetry." It continued for eleven months, and the discussion involved major issues such as "self-expression," "poetry and the spirit of our time," and the "foundation and direction of development of our new poetry."

1981: This was my most productive creative period; I wrote many poems that year.

1982: I married. In this year, for personal and public reasons, I stopped writing for almost three years. Some of my poems, such as "Assembly Line," "The Wall," "The Singing Iris," and "Two, Maybe Three Different Memories" were criticized. "Motherland, My Dear Motherland" won the "National Award for Outstanding

Works of Young Poets" for 1976-79. My first poetry collecttion, *A Boat with Two Masts*, was published by Shanghai Literature and Art Press and won the first "National Award for an Outstanding New Poetry Collection."

My other books include:

Selected Lyrics of Shu Ting and Gu Cheng. Fujian People's Press, 1982.
The Singing Iris, Sichuan Literature and Art Press, 1986.
Archaeopteryx, Haixia Literature and Art Press, Fujian, 1992.
The Mist of My Heart (40 essays written 1972-1987), Shanghai Literature and Art Press, 1988.
Carefree Life, Lujian Press, Fujian, 1994.

1983: I joined the national Writers' Association and was elected to its Board of Directors. I am also Vice President of the Fujian Writers' Association and of the Federation of Writers and Artists of Fujian. I am a member of the Fuijian Provincial Committee of the Chinese People's Political Consultative Conference.

*　　*　　*

I have travelled outside China nine times and visited more than ten countries. My poetry has been translated into more than twenty languages. Five collections have been published in foreign languages.

POEMS

From A Boat with Two Masts   (1982)

Morning Song at the Seashore

Early this morning I run to you, great sea,
to nestle my heart freely against your living, breathing breast...

Last night in a dream, I heard you calling me,
the way a mother calls her lost child.
When I awoke I heard your deep earthen singing,
that stirred to deeper and deeper solemnity,
indeed, called for wild devotion.
It shook the small island and my heart;
I could have sunk in a valley of your wave, with the island,
your surging waters drowning my heart;
each wave returned to the deep
to gather more powers
then burst up on the shore with a vengeance.
I rose in one motion, snapped the curtains open
  — the night's stars still glittered in the cold sky.
Wait for me; oh wait for me
Is it so you can't wait for the moment of dawn?

The morning breeze kissed the leaves of the beetle palm,
   till the dew ran;
when I arrived you were surpassingly gentle, even refined.
You smiled, you spoke softly,
You had calmed your tumult completely.
What remained seemed a little sad.
Only I knew
how the withered and rotten oak tree was broken,

though I won't tell anyone.
Watching a sail diminish steadily, I found myself crying,
the wind taking away for good your rhyming.
How should I keep myself from crying?
If I came too late,
If I lost track of the time last night;
If I am too young
    to break out the limitations of time and distance!

It will storm again;
please don't forget me
when your thunder
    shakes the sullen world.
I would sing the celebration in the tops of your high waves,
but no, I am of no special importance.
I'm willing to change into the smallest white bird,
a messenger that takes your call for freedom to the whole world.
Once I get wind of your secret meaning
I'll become resolute as stone,
being possessed by magic powers, unable to open my mouth again.
Let your storming perfect me till our voices are one.
Let your wild waves mold me to your shape and nature.
I will never falter
    nor retreat
    nor tremble with fear.
O great sea, please remember —
I am the true, the loyal daughter.

Early this morning I run to you, great sea,
my heart nestling freely against your living and breathing breast. . . .

January 9, 1975

Ah, Mama

Your pale fingers are combing the strands at my temples,
and how shall I help acting like the girl who was little
   grasping the front of your jacket.
Ah, Mama,
to keep your image from fading away gradually
when the morning sun breaks my dream into pieces of clouds,
I try not to open my eyes a long time.

I still hold your bright red scarf as a treasure,
fearing only repeated washing
   will blur your special fragrance.
Ah, Mama,
isn't the passing of time merciless?
I fear so much the fading of memories
I can hardly begin to open their scroll.

How I cried for you when I had a thorn,
and now that I have a veritable thorny cap on my head,
   I dare not
   utter even a groan.

Ah, Mama,
how often I look sadly upon your photograph;
even if my calling could penetrate the yellow earth,
how should I disturb your peaceful sleeping?

I still would not dare to present the gift of my love,
though I have written many songs,
   to flowers, to the sea, to dawns.
Ah, Mama,

my thoughts of you are sweet and gentle and deep,
not like the rapids or the waterfall, but also
like an ancient well obscured by trees and flowers that all but
   sing.

                                      August 1, 1975

Seeing a Friend off on an Autumn Evening

The first time your writing moved me
was during a steady Spring rain.
After tonight's good-byes, we'll likely not meet again.
That murmuring in the mulberry tree
is the unstirring wind of late Autumn.

You always saw yourself
as an old pine struck by lightning,
suffering burns and permanently damaged,
that could never, like the catkins flowering and drifting on the
   river bank,
take on an entirely new look every Spring.

I always wanted to be
a swan that journeys all the way from north to south,
making his way in the boundless sky.
I would not be the parrot, looking at its own shadow and
   lamenting its lot,
that can't leave its gilded cage nights or days.

It's our sad fate
and our pain in common
to think too much about life.
Our hearts, yes,
our hearts are often so heavy.

When will the old stump sprout new branches
and shake down deadwood and turn luxuriously green?
When will it always be Spring?
So that the exhausted soul is comforted
and needs no more to flee everywhere at once.

November 4, 1975

For You

I grip my wrists in pity for you,
out where moonlight flows over the gunwales,
out on the road in steady rains.
You hunch up your shoulders, shove your hands in your sleeves.
You seem afraid of the cold.
Your thoughts are deeply hidden.
You never know
when I walk beside you
with what pains I take each step.
If you are the fire,
I want to be the charcoal;
I want to say things like that to you, to comfort you,
but I don't dare.

I touch my forehead for joy
when the midnight lamp shines on your window,
for the image of you bending over your bookcase.
When you confess you've finally awakened
and Spring floods overflow
your mind's banks once more,
you never ask
the times I pass beneath your window
what is on my mind every night.
If you are the tree,
I will be the earth:
I want to call your attention to this,
but I don't dare.

November 11, 1975

On Mid-Autumn Moon Festival

On this island in August, on Mid-Autumn Moon Festival,
Bajiao banana trees swaying,
the longan fruit ripe and heavy,
I failed to notice the morning flowers and the evening's moon,
I've seen so many storms in recent years.
When my passions were most storm-tossed
my heart found no place to anchor.

My chosen path
has no rose blossoms,
but I have no regrets.
People find it easiest to dream in the moonlight,
to yearn for and understand gentle things.
But even when I try to alter my pulse to these ways,
the arrogance of being twenty-four gets in the way.

A strong shoulder would indeed be fine,
to lean my tired head on,
hands also
for support in the heaviest hours.
I understand, but
my life calls constantly,
never mind what's left for me and how much unhappiness I
    have to bear.

September 4, 1976

Wishes

I wish the wind would never again roar as it does tonight.
I wish the night would never again be so deep as it is tonight.
I wish your journey were not so dangerous,
I wish that the dangers don't destroy your courage.

I wish that tree on the cliff would wave to you for me.
I wish the stars would watch over you for me.
I wish each trident-plum would bless you on your way.
I wish that your steps not be delayed by hometown tearful faces.

I wish that you will not give up a tender heart in return for a hard one.
I wish that you will be immersed in love and not turn yourself into willful sword.
I wish that you will always be deeply and continuously in love.
I wish that the things you hate never get the signature of your love.

Nights are hidden in your shadow, like the grave, but also like the cradle.
The winds conceal your footprints, like funeral music, but are also a bugle sounding.
My heart is divided against itself,
half worried for you, half proud.

October 1976

Self-portrait

She is his little co-conspirator.

When he requires an answer, she says nothing;
when he requires silence, she laughs and makes noises
until his head swims.
She unbalances things;
she disregards doctrines;
she is a wilful little enchantress of the forest,
dancing wildly around him.

She is his little co-conspirator.

What he dreams of day and night she refuses him;
what he has never wanted in his life she offers freely.
She loves his tenderness, but won't admit it;
she's not yet got him and fears to lose him already.
She is a whirlpool and knows it, besides
creating other swirlings all around.
Who understands her magic!

She is his co-conspirator.

She won't come just because he calls, nor leave his waving
   her off.
She seems to want intimacy, but seems only; she wants to
   withdraw, but can't.
Sometimes she is an iceberg,
sometimes a sea of fire.

Often as not she is a song without words;
he listens, but can't tell the real from the made-up;
he thinks it over, but can't tell the sweet from the fiery.

But his, his . . .
she is his little co-conspirator.

April 1977

The Cypress Vine Dreams of the Moon

If you were rain,
I would grow mightily in a moment;
if you embraced me,
I would spiral into the sky.

If you didn't leave as hurriedly,
we would certainly be entwined in heaven.

April 1977

April Dusk

In the April dusk
flows one green melody after another,
winding deeply into canyons,
wandering in the air.
When your soul is so filled with echoings
why look so hard for it elsewhere!
If you need to sing, just do it, please,
but softly, yes, softly and gently.

April dusks
yield fragments of memories lost and found again.
Perhaps there was a rendezvous
that had not been remembered until now.
Perhaps there were the passions of a love
that couldn't make any promises.
So if you want to, cry. Go ahead; let the tears
flow and flow, silently.

May 6, 1977

This Is Also "All"
— In response to a young friend's poem "All"

Not all the grand trees
   have been broken by the storm,
not all seeds
   fail to find some soil to root in;
not all true feelings
   are lost in some desert of the soul,
not all dreams
   are willing to be broken.

No, not everything,
as you described.

Not all fires
   burn only one's own
   but not a way for others;
not all the stars
   merely prove the onset of night
   but can't shine till the morning;
not all songs
   merely go in one ear and out the other
   and don't live on in the heart.

No, not everything
as you described.

Not all shouts fail of an echo,
not all losses cannot be made-up;
not every abyss means final doom,
it's not all doom over the heads of the weakened;
not all souls

    can be trampled to spoil in the mud,
not every consequence
    is tears or blood, or void of joy.

Every Now carries within it a seed of the future;
every Future grows out of its own past.
Take hope, and struggle for your hopes.
Please, take this All on your own shoulders.

July 25, 1977

Motherland, My Dear Motherland

I am that old water-wheel in ruins on the river's bank,
that for hundreds of years past spun a weary song:
I am the blackened miner's lamp on your forehead,
lighting not quite the tunnel where you grope for history.
I am the dried, empty spikes of rice in the field, the potholed
   road,
the barge on a silted shoal,
the tow-ropes
   cutting into your shoulder.
   — O motherland!

I the poverty,
I the sorrow —
I have been for generations
   the bitter pain of your hope;
I have been the flower in the sleeve of the flying Apsaras*
My beloved motherland!

                                April 20, 1979

---

*Apsaras is a figure in the wall paintings of the Dunhuang Grottes, Gansu, ca. 366-ca.1300.

The Cry of a Generation

I will not presume to appeal
to my own misfortune.
The end of youth for me,
the spiritual deformity,
the countless, sleepless nights,
leave painful memories.
One after another I overturned the wrong;
one after another I shook off the spiritual bonds,
until in my heart was left
one vast ruin . . .
But I was standing then,
surveying a broad horizon,
and no one by any means
can put me down ever again.

If I lay in a common grave of "revolutionary martyrs,"
the inscription on the stone will be erased by green;
if I have experienced life behind bars,
argued with handcuffs about the nature of the law,
if I am haggard or pallid,
doing the hardest labor one does for a crime,
   time without probation,
if any of these were mine, it were merely
my misfortune —
I have forgiven others already;
after all my tears and anger
I have calmed down.

But, to the fathers of children
and to the children of fathers,
to those under monuments all over the country,

the secret accusations will not make people tremble ever again.
For those pictures of all the homeless sleeping in the streets
will not shame our eyes into no place to hide.
For you innocent children hundreds of years from now
won't have to solve a historical riddle left for you.
For the sake of the stagnation of our history,
for our part of the rugged path our nation has taken,
for the purity of our skies
    and the straightness of our roads,
I am asking for the truth.

January – February 1980

To My Generation

If they were seen from far out in the universe,
they would be seen as one small star.
On earth,
they would be seen as one light.
They are not afraid of appearing very, however, small;
they only want to do what they can.

It's because they are not recognized
they are particularly brave and believable.
Even if they fall down and break into pieces, each a teardrop,
the whole, re-visioned world
will remain everywhere
a durable and lasting echo.

Their cause was opening a virgin land of mind;
they walked into prohibited territory; perhaps
they will have sacrificed themselves there.
Still, they will have left their conflicting trails
for those who come after,
and signed besides the necessary papers for their entry.

                                           May 1980

After the Storm Is Over

— Commemorating the seventy-two people who died in an accident on an drilling rig

1

In Bohai Bay,
where columns of dark clouds hang down, memorial couplets
become my seventy-two brothers.

In the paths Spring takes every year,
the waves and the last of winter plotted together
to stop the breath of seventy-two souls.

2

Seventy-two faces burning with expectations
were unable to find the sun
on any horizon.
Seventy-two pairs of steel shoulders
were also unable to hold up
their sinking world.

They went down into the waters like a dropped anchor.
The storm won —
that time.

3

Seventy-two sons
made their fathers' last years sad.
Seventy-two fathers
became the lost memories of their little sons.

Those who watched it happen out in the sea,
   from the beaches,
finally hung their heads in helpless grief,
like question marks, one by one,
that remain, erect and unyielding in the harbor at sunset,
that will endure in all the histories of our seas.

On their watchful tower
the flag flies at half-mast.

4

The typhoon passed a long time ago
but the drowning cries of the seventy-two men,
so long kept between the lines,
threaded their winding ways
to microphones finally
and echoed loudly off the walls of justice.

In mid-summer
hundreds of thousands of hearts
suddenly knew a chill.

5

And no, I am not extemporizing
an ancient Roman tragedy.
I want you to consider these with me:
The selling price for my grandfather
was two liters of millet.
My father, for the abstract word "Humanity"
threw himself against the barricades of the enemy's block
   house.

And now it is our fortune to be worth more than Grandfather,
two rivets and one machine more.

6

Who said a life is a leaf,
and even as it withers the tree lives?
Who said a life is no more than sea spray
and even after it disappears the sea rolls on forever as it will?
Who said that if they have been declared heroes
their deaths are to be forgotten?
Who said that all the modernizations of human lives
required this kind of blood-sacrificial rite?

7

I pray, when the siren in my factory blows,
my mother will have no need to worry about me.
I pray the treatment meted out to me
will not misshape younger hearts.
I pray I can learn to live and work
for others the same as for myself.
I pray, should I be killed,
no one's heart need tremble about why.
I fervently pray, finally,
poets in the future
will not have to know this powerless anger,
as when the seventy-two
pairs of eyes turning to sea weed and red coral
watch intimately over their pens.

August 6, 1980, Beijing

A Love Poem to the Land

I love my home ground, the way
I love my reticent father.

Ah, you life-giving, pulsing, lively land,
the yeast of our sweat permeates you;
beneath the rugged plough and bare feet
    panting softly,
compelled by your own inner energy
    rising and falling in hills,
you shoulder bronze statues, monuments and museums
but reserve the rights to final judgements of faults.
Oh my home ground,
frozen, muddy, cracked like a tortoise shell!
Oh my home ground,
harried, indignant, generous and strict!
That gives me the very color of my skin, and my language,
that gives me wisdom and strength.

I love my home ground, the way
I love my gentle and considerate mother.

Ah, you bountiful, kissed-by-the-sun home ground,
so generous and free with the milk of the land,
taking layer after layer of fallen leaves,
then nourishing crop after crop of fresh growth,
forsaken repeatedly
but never betraying in return;
yielding our very sounds and hues and designs
though you are called, simply, mud.
Oh my home ground, my
pitch-dark, bloody, and shining white home ground!

Oh my home ground, my
lush, lonely, and severe land,
giving me to love and to hate,
giving me to suffer and to exult!

My father gave me an endless dream;
my mother gave me a gentle and real heart;
this, my poem is
    a restless, yearning tree
that pours out its love to the land day and night,
    whose love can never change.

                                          October 1980

On Your Going-away: A Gift

In one's lifetime there must surely be
    many train-stops
and I want there to be at each of them
a light burning in fog.
Because there is no shoulder here
    to shield me from the whistling wind
to use his freezing fingers
    to tuck-in my white scarf,
I want there to be a light, like tonight.
Even though and because a snow storm has sealed
    all the passes
someone will always be beginning a long journey.

We are always doomed to lose track eventually,
    for long days and nights;
I need only
    a peaceful morning,
a wrinkled handkerchief
    opened upon a damp bench,
you opening your blue notebook
beneath the mango tree still whispering last night's rain,
you rising to leave after writing lines for a poem
I get only from memory,
from your path by the lake
    and your footprints and your silhouette.

If there were no separations or reunions,
if one did not dare to bear happiness or suffering,
what would be the meaning of one's soul?
How could such living be called life?

                                August 4, 1980

Untitled

I leaned from my balcony railing, following
you walking away through a lush growth of flowers and trees.
Wait! How far are you going?
I rushed down the stairs, to get in front of you.
"Are you afraid?" you asked;
I fingered around a button on your shirt silently.
Yes, I am afraid,
but I wouldn't tell you why.

We were walking once along a quiet bend in the river,
an evening that invited feelings, a comfortable one.
I held your arm as we strolled casually.
We passed osmanthus trees, one after another.
"Are you happy?" you asked;
I looked up and the stars swam toward me.
Yes, I was happy,
but I wouldn't tell you why.

There was a scene of you bending over my desk
to look at a few lines of one of my little poems,
my face reddening as I put the poem away.
You congratulated with serious kindness,
"You are in love."
I sighed in silence.
Yes, I am in love,
but I wouldn't tell you who he is.

October 1980

From Selected Lyrics of Shu Ting and Gu Cheng (1982)

To a Poet of Fairy Tales

You believed in the fairy tales you wrote
until you were a dark blue flower in a fairy tale.
Your eyes edited-out
sick trees, crumbling walls,
rusted and broken iron railings.
With only simple signs,
you gathered a team of stars, milk vetch and long-horned
    grasshoppers and
rode off to an unpolluted, never-never land.
Giddy-up there!

The heart, perhaps, is very, very small,
but the world is large, indeed.

Nevertheless, people believed you.
They believed, after a rain in the panes,
millions of suns are to be seen hanging.
They preferred sweet mulberries, and a fishing pole out over a
    river.
They believed clouds twine around the tails of kites
shaking loose from so many memories
the dust of time.
Your voice comes of a pure, silvery time
where one speaks with one's dream.

This world, perhaps, is very, very small,
but the realm of the heart is large, indeed.

                                                    1980

? . !

So, it's true
you would wait for me,
till the seeds in my basket are all scattered,
till I've sent all the wandering wild bees home,
till all the sails, the villages and the factories
    are all lighted by lamps and torches,
till I've read all the lighted and dim windows, one by one,
    and finished talking with the bright and gloomy souls,
till the main highway has turned into a song,
till love is alive in daylight;
and should the great Milky Way set us apart
you would still wait for me, patiently,
making a raft of fidelity.

So, it's true
you will never alter your word,
even when my gentle hands grow rough
    or when my red cheeks turned pale,
though I blew the flute till I bled
    and still the icy snows did not melt away,
though the lash chased me with only awful cliffs ahead,
though the darkness got me before the dawn
    and I and the earth sank together,
though I had no chance to release your way "the bird of
  yearning":

in any case, your waiting and your loyalty
are the price
of my sacrifice.

If it's so, let them
fire away,
I will cross an open field deliberately
toward you, always toward you,
the wind weaving my tresses.
I will be the lily in your passion's storm.

At Dusk

I said I heard soft steps behind us;
you said it's the breeze kissing the path I walk.

I said the stars are fireworks rioting in heaven;
you said they are my eyelashes touched with pollen.

I said the clusters of new chrysanthemums had closed sleepy eyes;
you said the night blooms had opened their hearts petal after petal.

I said this late Spring night teems with life;
you said this dusk reels with intoxication.

April 27, 1977

On the Painting
"A Young Lady at the Spring"

It wells up from the heart, drop after drop,
and flows toward the far-away in a winding course;
so two limpid solitudes
are fulfilled
in one shining dream.

At once the cries of geese arouse the passions of the mountains
so that even the forest desires to take wings and fly away.
The eyes in the ripples
and the ripples in the eyes
are perhaps both not simply calm.

Returning in Dream

A lily stalk I knew so well
   (its petals falling on my sill)
  — led me to confusion.

Somebody's breath seeming a draught at my ear
   (a face deeply buried in hands)
  — stopped my breathing.

Even a simple etude
   (Mother's hands, the wind on the windows)
  — and ah, I can cry again.

Because of such specifics, ignored,
because of such revelations reunderstood,
it returns to me — my passion,
  — as fragments of poetry.

To the Legendary Lady of Huian

A wildfire burns in the distance,
the distance in your amber eyes.

Silver baubles from an ancient tribe
hang from your soft wrist.
If one can't confirm you will be happy, your girl-dreams
scatter gradually to the ocean, like dandelions.
Ah, the ocean sprays are eternal.

Naturally, you don't like recounting your suffering.
Nor can it mean your suffering is finished for always.
When the songs of the bamboo flute and the lute
awaken sorrow in twilight
you bite softly the scarf's corner at your mouth.

Graciously you wait between the sea and the sky
and no one notices your naked feet
cut by the rocks and bitter sands.
And this is why, on the covers and inside the magazines,
you are merely part of the scenery and a myth.

At a Dank Little Station

A breeze perhaps, if so, indistinct,
rain drops uncertain, too, now and then:
it is late Autumn in the south again.

A young girl runs toward me joyfully,
then turns and runs away, disappointed.
Her bouquet topples on the bend of her arm.

Who is her intended?
The station platform is empty;
the lights glisten in rain.

Then my train starts, slowly,
beneath the orange halos of lights;
a white silk handkerchief flashed past.

                              November 5, 1977

The Wall

I was unable to rebel against this wall;
I only wished to do so.

Who am I?
What is this? It is very possibly
merely my own skin gradually aging.
It feels no cold rain nor chilly wind;
it doesn't acknowledge the fragrance of orchids.
It is also possible that I am merely an
   Asiatic plantain of some kind,
a parasite decorating
the bed of some muddy creek.
If this is incidental, it is also inevitable.

Still, in the evening, the wall begins to move,
stretching forth its soft pseudopod,
squeezing me,
forcing me to take all kinds of other shapes.
I panic and escape into the street;
I find the same nightmare I know
hanging at everyone's heels.
One after another come the flinching eyes,
one after another the cold walls.

Ah, I see now,
I must first reject
my own compromises with that wall
to battle my fears out in the world.

October 31, 1980

A White Swan
— Killed in Beijing

" Don't tell me
    this is a polluted brook, (Nature's ballroom indeed!)
    that I can nest on your shoulders, one after another.
Don't simply bury me
    when merchants can use the value of my feathers, scholars
        can fix me in a zoological taxonomy,
    lovers can make me their symbol, advertise me to tourists.

Swans, don't sleep too deeply nights.
Don't trust the silence; silence can be filled with deceit.
People, if you can't put a stop to it, at least
turn your back to it.
Don't make me see
your anger and indifference whiling away the time.

Don't call to my companions to stay.
    When tree branches rise with the sun in morning mist,
        let the gun shots teach them how to choose freedom once
            more.
Don't make me into a specimen,
    my bullet-pierced wings curling into warm blood,
    drops mixing in the dust, cooling to embers.
Don't cry, little one;
if someday you want to become
    a cloud,
    a bounding, dancing bunny,
    the white sailboat on your notebook,
don't forget me.

                                                1981

From The Singing Iris   (1986)

The Heart Has Its Own Law

Dying, for a flower,
is worth it.
Beneath indifferent wheels
and crude boots,
Spring rainbows
were overshadowed in everyone's eyes.
No one could stop it
and there was no place to tell the suffering.
So, dying for protest
was worth it.

Being silent behind words
is worth it;
it is far better than a tide
falling in avalanche;
words, I mean,
tightly held behind the lips,
that draw on lifelong courage and honesty:
such words can't be spoken.
Being silent so, and not betraying,
is worth it.

To be totally faithful to one's promise?
Bear loneliness to offer as one's only tribute,
yes. One ought not spend life too freely.
On the contrary, each heart knows its own law.

If needs be,
we can die many times.
Our silences, turned to stone,
like outcroppings,
show how long time has been flying.
But remember
the strongest protest
and the most courageous honesty
are not better than — surviving
while speaking out.

          January 13, 1976

"I Love You"

Whose eyes brimmed with tears to write randomly
these three words in the beach sand?

Who cherished so someone, or quietly hoped,
and formed the declaration out of seven-colored shells?

The one who came along later must have been a girl,
who added a bunch of chrysanthemums tied in her red handkerchief.

And so, people passing here
are, of course, possessed by a mysterious longing for love.

                                            1976

Words for a Stele

I am on the earth's axis;
I am the settling out of History's long river.
After the quake's violent sculpting and expulsions of molten
   rock.
I am born, Asia rising.

People, rising after me,
insist on what you want to be, please express yourselves
   on the hopes and longings of generations.

October, 1978

An Old House

Sunlight, like a snake,
moves at the chilled, shady base of the wall.
The blinds are closed tight.
Faces that once opened to the great sea
have all fallen to sleep and will not waken.
The shiny, smooth, carved railings
and the stairs now cluttered with fallen leaves
are pages in memories no one will open again.
Only a Christmas tree and cedar boughs
wait in ready silence,
but no one is coming.

Only if the breeze implores
will the hungry and thirsty branches dance.
Cornflowers now move in unison, in rhythm,
like a girl stirred
by the least sound
of air moving.
Deep in this enormous house is an Italian clock.
Last light shivers
and fills the sunset.
Up along the winding trail by the garden, who
is it coming as if called, and goes slowly away?

A desolated, forgotten heart,
a long gone fashionable song.

December 1980, Gulangyu

To a Friend Going Abroad

My days of worrying about you are over
and it's not yet time to share your victories.
After the clinking moonlight toasts
joined with the waves of blood warm with wine
I can hardly believe
    you will wander a strange land; I can hardly believe
    you've abandoned your small island where flowers bloom
        always.
I can hardly believe
    your humble wooden door deep in the alley won't open
        for me,
    that no one, jacket fluttering in the wind,
    will send me all the way to the harbor quay.

I don't believe in separations and I don't believe in forgetting.
I don't believe in shadows hiding in dark corners,
    eyeing prey like a tiger.

So long as you have a moment of freedom,
let that moment be all.
Perhaps one pursues a thing for life
and finally finds the pursuit was everything.
Sometimes one passes through the Arc de Triumph
without knowing it.

The steam whistle knits in the heart a longing for home;
home waters flow through cooling the fingers.

Goddess Peak

Among those waving colorful handkerchiefs
whose hand is that suddenly pulled back
and capped over her eyes?
And when they all go back inside, who
is the one who remains in the stern?
Dresses and shirts had blown freely as the whitecap clouds,
the Yangtze rolling
  both loud
  and deep.

The goddess's dream of love returning is a beautiful sorrow
surpassing generations now, here and beyond.
But could a heart
really turn to stone?
For a chanced glimpse of a distant crane
she misses always the surprised joy of Spring River moonlight.

Along the shore now
a flood of pale-gold chrysanthemums and glossy privets
spread a new rebellion:
  Better to cry away one night on a lover's shoulder
  than be the stone star on a famous cliff a thousand years.

June 1981, on the Yangtse River

A Poem I Wish I Had Read to My Mother

The melancholy strains of your *qin*
   have faded away
      from the stream of tears in my dream.
Your final smile,
   like the last leaf
      high in my misty branches,
         trembles in eternity.

Ah, is there no path
on which I can come to you quietly? Mama.
Life and starlight
were taken for good from your image
that stormy afternoon
your eyes showed your last struggles
   to make
      the palm's grand plume.

Now, years later, I see
   your message left on the window glass,
   your breast filled with protests at being destroyed.
Ah, must it be so no matter which way the winds blow
they can't carry my singing to you? Mama,
I pray all those you forgave
will try again themselves for your mercy.

                                            August 4, 1981

A Monument for My Mother

She ebbed away like the tide.
The night was almost gone; the moon and stars were dim
and wearily
    I fell asleep on her pillow.
I dreamed a tallow tree, sunlight in the surface of a lake
and a smile in her lips,
    sometimes tight-lipped, sometimes invisible.
She ebbed away like the tide. My Mama:
Darkness gathered around her,
but I was sleeping; a breeze
rustled
and scattered a dried rose all over
her sickbed.

She ebbed away like the tide,
never to return, like the sea.
The days that touched her now wander freely;
a voice calls her all day, tearfully.
The sweet-orange she planted is fully grown now
and its fruit, souvenirs of her,
    to whom shall I give it?
She ebbed away like the tide. My Mama.
How sad I am now
I couldn't stay awake that night.
For all the powers of youth and love though,
could I have brought her back at dawn?
Let me now, while so many hearts are so close to the spring,
for all mothers,
establish a simple monument.

                                                August 1981

Fled to the Moon
— Chang E stole Emperor Hou Yi's medicine of immortality and fled to the moon

The dream of Spring forever was crystal clear, as are you.
But where did you both so quickly disappear?
In any case, you did care nothing for consequences, simply
   flinging
yourself into the abyss beyond the living.
And though the moon accepted your rebellion
loneliness a thousand years was your only friend.

And not even the tallest peaks
could be chains holding you down?
Did you fly so far so lightly?
The sheer sweetness in your faint music,
through a thousand years' performances,
   is good as eternal.

September 4, 1981

White Palms

In clear-cut lands,
two white palms
shrug-off the memories of the axes chopping away.
Among the wild grasses and stumps and stakes,
two white palms
revise a last movement into a bright and splendid prelude.

Beams of sunlight dance together
like downy bees,
the bunched fronds and new leaves dancing, too,
flaming and shimmering in all different motions.
The mountains give all the colors in the wheel
back to the blue-white sky.

You proclaim love powerfully
but the world around you answers in silence.
Your bases are firm
but your life is dancing —
until the sunset
shines on the red swallows in all your greenery.

What word could be more clear
than two white palms chosen here by the wilderness.

October, 1981
Wuyi Mountain

In Memory of Grandmother

There is that memory that has to file a form
    when a relative passes away;
there is that that retouches in red a name
    once a year (and it quickly fades);
there is that that can't quit talking too loud
    so no one forgets the size of the inheritance,
and there is that that makes a folktale of grandma,
    to tell the grandchildren "once upon a time".

There is that memory that is all tears,
    retaking pictures of gone days over and over;
there is that that is voiceless and still,
    like the shadows hiding songbirds here and there;
there is that that is a concealed path
    one wanders in and there regrets alone,
and there is that that is filled with the bitter and the sweet
    days such as Grandpa lived, and so he couldn't live long.

Ah, thank goodness
the old ones I'm thinking of live in memories
    that are none of these.

                                                       May 5, 1984

From Archaeopteryx (1992)

A Concert at St. Mary's

Be baptized here
and be reborn
in the arms of the Madonna.
Don't look up;
the harmonies flowing over you
are actually
waves from your heart,
and you are suddenly transparent,
    as suddenly chilled to the bone.

You don't need to go into details if
you were unable to name particulars.
The pure, empty, boundless sky
is dazzled in its own reflections.
The blond, the brown-haired one, the dark head,
the honest one, the mean one, the vicious one,
in this moment,
are sheep in one of Bach's great melodies.

                              November 1985, Berlin

Forget-Me-Nots

Blue flames
dance in the flowing ice of the characters.
My little book slips from my hand
and before it reaches the ground
I have already
run away with someone, happily.

Shall I say, "because of you"?
Only you?
    Should we meet by chance tomorrow,
    pages of a diary of many years,
    a letter without an ending,
    a silent name in the closing,
and birthday flowers kept fresh by memories
will have lived through to this moment, longer than youth's
    bamboo fences.

In my heart
this happened hundreds of years ago,
ages ago.
Since then I've outgrown soul after soul.
So why am I always startled to new life
by these three characters?

Forget-me-nots,
forget-me-nots:
who forgot me?
And whom did I forget?

                                    July 17, 1986

Where Zen Is Cultivated

Sit calmly, until cliffs of a thousand feet are formed
facing the ocean.

A woman carrying water winds toward you,
the sunset bound around her bare feet.
The grass paths she walks are beaten white
and make more marvelous her golden silks.
    You water merely my shadow;
    green and luxurious are your deepest desires.

The wind brushes the sky lightly;
silver and golden little beetles
search with their feelers, that one after another
break beside me.
Don't sparkle for me, stars,
that I am ground to bits by the mills of this world,
I gather in myself my own light and give it back to life.

I am facing an ocean
but where is the ocean?
Are the waves that flow from the Japanese copper flutes
the same as these
colorless, flavorless, thought-dissolving, world-dissolving
  waters?

Sit again,
until real quiet fills you.
Consider the small grass that holds back the precipice.
Let your spirit go,
until all the ridges and gullies are gone,
and only then,
come back to even ground.
                    July 1986, San Francisco

Shui Xian*

"Women change like rivers and catkins"
goes the old Chinese saying
that has sent many a fiery heart into internal exile
and led women themselves into lives of wandering.
Declaring women are made of clear waters
the Prince of Yihong became a monk
and since then generations have relived his Dream of the Red
    Chamber.

The south is full of these flowers;
they're wholesaled and retailed to the remotest window sills.
Add a jar of clear water and
it shoots green leaves and jade stems in the golden vase on
    the silver tray.
A pity it surely is its fragrant soul
can't bear the many cuts and the carvings of the knife.

When the heart dries up
one irrigates it with one's own tears.
Without tears, the world turns desolate and arid.
Women's love
covers actually four-fifths of the earth.

Luo Sheng, the river goddess, became the waters,
as did Xiang Fei;
nowadays
girls deny their roots and their crowns of hair are washed in
    these legends.
But

---

*Shui Xian (literally "water fairy") a narcissus; its mature bulb is carved in a special way and then the bulb is placed in water and produces a flower.

women who stand at the rivers for mirrors, however, grow
   lithe,
and unfold in wave after wave,
and their men are drawn into their waters steadily.

In Fujian, in the south, so many girls are named for
   Shui Xian
if you call
"Shu Xian, it's time for dinner!",
all the young ladies in the street will answer at once.

                                        December 2, 1987

A Room with Two Beds*

1.

Would that the white curtains hung still and low
around the two sleepers, fragrant lilies,
and in dreams their reunion flows gently, sweetly,
like the waters of the Ganges.

Except that the blue bird in West Berlin
and the red-beaked one in the Pearl estuary
are migratory, flying north and south,
passing over this dreamland,
becoming, so to speak, one bird with two tongues.
Their cries are separated songs;
their laughters are at separate matters.

2.

Two beds are like a pair of big shoes;
one going about surely means lameness of some kind,
something lost, anyway.

Side by side, the beds are sister ships;
their burdens unloaded,
they float languidly.
A sea of moonlight
is thereby vouched-safe.

---

*A hotel room the poet shared with a woman poet friend at a conference.

3.

Children's tears are a chain of pearls;
you can map the weathers in husbands' faces;
home is a long distance telephone number;
but however empty, however lonesome her heart,
a woman is always busy with living.

A room
belonging to her only
appealed to the English lady writer
for refining the worlds of women.
We give ourselves into "slavery" willingly;
children are flowers in our arms,
a husband is a warm and cozy old garment,
home is pots and pans, needles, a mop,
    four walls to block the wind,
and the family is a treasury of feelings;
sometimes we take something out, sometimes put in.

A small room
of one's own,
that one we hoped for day and night —
it finally takes shape in our
squared windows
and a space made by dividing lines.

4.

These days the grand rivers make few digressions,
   the small ones many.
The Spring floods are already safely behind us
It's years since I had hung up my brush.
Tianlin, the pangs of missing you, like the lily's petals,
fall one after another,
and the yellow-eyed, red-cheeked calamus blossoms
multiply on the veranda of the room with the two beds,
where I wait anxiously in the rain, long after dark.

January 31, 1988

Guanyin, Drop by Drop*

Your face is so fine and elegant
not the least speck of dust sticks to it.
Your shoulders are such musical lines
even a glance from behind
might bring a kingdom to ruin.
Trouble is endless in the human world
and yet your eyes and your nose consider only your own heart.
Is it so
you've already trampled under bare feet all joy and misery?

I take her seated position
the four walls open, my lotus,
and the sky fills suddenly with the wisdom of eyes
that must be closed and yet are closed not at all.
There are neither
eternal questions to delve
　nor
eternally unreachable answers.
The only thing heard
is Heaven echoing
　　tick,
　　tick,
smooth drops of wisdom
falling from He Chaozong's fingers,**
that have passed through these thousands of years
and are still warm.

　　　　　　　　　　　　　　　　1988

---

*Guanyin: a Bodhisattva in traditional Buddhism who attained enlightenment but chose to remain in the world in order to help mankind.

**He Chaozong was a master of porcelain figures of the Ming dynasty at Dehua, Fujian. Copies of his popular masterpiece, *The Dripping Guanyin*, now in the British Museum, continue to be produced by Fujian craftsmen.

PROSE

People, Please Understand Me (1980)

PEOPLE, please understand me.

I have never considered myself a true poet. I know that I will never be a thinker (though how willing I am). My experiences have taught me that people have a crying need for respect, trust, and warm relationships. I want to try my best to express in my poetry my deep concern about the human condition.

We must clear away the obstacles in our path; people must put aside their masks. I believe people can understand each other because one can always find a way that leads to the other's heart.

ESSAYS

Life, Books, and Poetry
— and to answer letters from my readers (1980)

ONE day when I was four years old, I was at the doorway of our house with Grandpa. He held up his finger to attract my attention and then began to teach me a beautiful poem:

> On Tomb-Sweeping Festival day the rain pours down
> As I travel this road, lonely and distraught.
> I ask where is the wine shop
> The buffalo boy points to a village hidden in the apricot grove.*

He said it once again and then went into the house to get a cigarette. When he came back he was amazed to hear me saying the poem's last two lines as I jumped back and forth across the threshold. He decided right then to let me go with my Grandma to her "Wipe Out Illiteracy" class so I could begin to learn to read. Whenever Grandma's class had a test I would stand on a stool in front of their big table and give hints about the new characters, shouting, "Don't worry, Grandma. I'll save you!" The teacher just smiled and ignored my antics. She probably never thought that Grandma's good scores on the tests had anything to do with a naughty four-year-old girl.

When I was in third grade I began to read books other than my textbooks, and I read so much that my classroom seat was changed from the back of the room to the front row because of the strain I was putting on my eyes. My craze for reading began to worry my family. Mama would search until she found me hiding in a hallway, behind a door, or under the clothes-

---
*Tu Mu (803-52), "Qing Ming" (Tomb-Sweeping Festival).

rack — allways with a book. My uncles and aunts all like to read and they had good collections of books in their rooms, which I raided despite their best efforts to keep me from getting at those books. Later, when I was in middle school, I was proud that my library card listed lots of foreign books. When a classmate asked me, "Why do you read so many foreign books?" I answered, "I've already read all the Chinese books." Then my school class held a rectification meeting to criticize me for looking down on native culture, but in those days the so-called "Chinese bocks" were ones with titles like "A Guerrilla Unit behind Enemy Lines". My Grandma told me bed-time stories every night from the classics, so I knew well *The Journey to the West*, *The Three Kingdoms*, and *Strange Stories from a Chinese Studio*.

I always earned good grades in composition. I remember how happy I was when my fifth-grade teacher enthusiastically praised my very first composition, titled "A Day in My Hometown," and read it to the class. She wrote on the blackboard a dozen of my exuberant phrases, like "mottled shadows of trees" and "having a fantastic idea." It seemed a pity to me that I would have to put so much effort into correcting my bad habit of using words indiscriminately. In junior-middle one, I won first prize in a composition contest, but then the next year my final examination in composition was given a failing grade for having what the examiner labelled as "petty bourgeois sentimentality." Fifteen years later my poetry would suffer a similar denouncement.

When I was thirteen, I had often recited in public, but only the texts that my teachers assigned — never poetry, so it is still something of a mystery to me how I managed to write my first poem, which was published in my school magazine that year. That poem, "A Thousand Mountains Colored Red," had five characters in each line and was written in a mixture of classical and vernacular language. I remember how very pleased I was at the time.

Even though the "cultural revolution" ended my schooling after only two years in junior middle school, my education has been an important foundation for my writing. It gave me an interest in language and the self-discipline to continue learning five characters each day after I had been sent to the countryside. That helped me to be more flexible in my expression, but I am also aware of the need to guard against the fatal weakness of falling in love with language without being sensitive enough about how to use it. Tolstoy correctly insisted, "Let the poet find the only correct way of using the only correct word."

My school years were a kaleidoscope of summer camps, biology field trips, and singing contests. In my dreams the future shone in bright colors on a distant horizon. It seemed that if I just kept moving forward my arms would finally hold those faraway rosy clouds.

My first friends were my teachers. I followed my Biology teacher jumping into a damp, abandoned tomb to collect moss, and overcame my fear of darkness. Every day after lunch I went to the music room and held my breath in admiration while I watched my music teacher's agile fingers, which reminded me of a bubbling brook. After evening classes my Geography teacher often walked me to the street corner, under the starlight of Polaris; I can still recall the comforting weight of his hand on my shoulder. I cried bitterly when the teacher in charge of my class was transferred to a remote mountain region as punishment for using teaching methods that were too motherly. But, teacher, if they accused you of teaching us with love, that was in what you wrote on the blackboard, and that was what was in your eyes and in the sound of your voice when you tutored us after class. If love was the soul of your teaching, then, it too is the subject of my struggle and of my poetry.

"Thump." Something fell on my shoulder. I reached up and found it was a bullet, still warm to the touch. Outside, my Red Guard comrades-in-arms, wearing their red arm bands, were storming the Physical Science Building while I was reading Victor Hugo's *1793*.* That novel had attack and defense, suffering and struggle, humiliation and anger, but also truth, goodness, and beauty. I tried to immerse myself totally in that other world that was unfolded by foreign literature, especially works of Balzac, Tolstoy, and Mark Twain. But I could not escape my nightmares of heavy wooden signboards hung from steel wire that dripped with blood from where it brutally cut into the back of a victim's neck. The humiliation in their eyes, of those people whom I respected so much, became an endless, dark stream of tears. I would awaken with a start, bathed in sweat. Then I would pack up some clothes and food to take to my father, who was in jail. It was like walking into another nightmare filled with scorn and hate.

The glossy gold plating on the surface of life was gradually peeling off, exposing its ugly bumps and pits. Only books could offer satisfaction.

In 1969, like everyone in my generation, I packed up my English textbooks — and with them my dream of going to college — and my book of Pushkin's poetry in my suitcase and went to a strange place. At the station the sound of the train whistle tore my heart to shreds. There was crying everywhere on the platform and in the trains. I gazed at the outline of the mountains in remote western Fujian and thought of the Russian December revolutionaries who had been sent into exile — they must not have cried. I would finish my education in a "college" like Gorki's.** Life continually taught lessons to my naive delusions. But the "college" of real life taught me more than a formal university would have.

A crowd and I packed into a shabby old temple to listen to guitar playing filled with sad homesickness. I sat on a sandy

---

*Victor Hugo, *Quatre-Vingt-Treize (Ninety-three)*, published in 1874.
**The Russian writer Maxim (Maksim) Gorki (Gorky, 1868-1936), orphaned at an early age, had little formal education.

inlet under dim moonlight, singing with my companions "My Home is by the Sungari River." I lay in the fragrant straw and listened to a dog barking far away in the cold, with silent tears running down my cheeks.... Even the most difficult days of my exile would leave nostalgic memories. Like many of my pals, I travelled from one mountain village to another, and was warmly welcomed by the student settlers. The things I saw and the stories I heard, and those familiar but remote faces densely mark my memory like the stars studding the night sky. I swore to write a novel, like Ai Wu's *Record of My Journey to the South*, as eye-witness to the victimization of my generation.

I started to write because of all that.

I kept a diary every day during those three years, but just before I returned to the city I burned three thick books of those diaries. Fortunately, some pages survived and later were published in the first issue of *Rongshu Congkan (Banyan Series)*.

I wrote out copies of poems that I admired. That served as a kind of training in poetry. I was fascinated with Tagore's poetry and He Qifan's *Yyan (Foretell)*. In my notebook there were poems of Byron, Mickiewicz, and Keats, as well as Yin Fu, Zhu Ziqing, and Ying Xiuren.*

I should also mention letters. When I was in the countryside, writing and reading letters was a great pleasure. I still remember how anxious I was for the first glimpse of the mailman's green bag as I waited on the path outside the village, and how I would rush to open a letter and read it right there at the bridge. I had written a short poem to a friend:

Just start your journey, dear girl,
the course of life is wide and free.

---

*Rabindranath Tagore (1861-1941; Bengali); He Qifan (1912-77), *Foretell* (1945); George Gordon, Lord Byron (1788-1824); Adam Mickiewicz (1798-1855), Polish nationalist Romantic poet; John Keats (1795-1821); Yin Fu (1909-31); Zhu Ziqing (1898-1948); and Ying Xiuren (1900-33).

And after the poem began to circulate among young people I started to gain some literary friends who would send me books that they found interesting. I remember staying inside after work every day for a month reading Franz Mehring's biography of Karl Marx.* I read all the annotations in four volumes of the *Selected Works of Mao Zedong*,** though I don't worship idols. I also read, with considerable difficulty, philosophical works such as *The Dialogues of Plato* and *A Brief Education in Aesthetics* — and then forgot them without difficulty. My literary friends emphasized the classics, so I read classical literature. My favorites were the *Ci*-poetry of Li Qingzhao and Qing Guan and classical prose.

In May 1971 I visited the bridge at Shanghang, Fujian, with a friend who was a college student majoring in Political Economy. He talked about poetry and politics with me for three days, and everything he said would have put him on a list of antirevolutionaries. He was sure that I could be a poet, and he insisted that if writing does not express the writer's own genuine beliefs it can never be great literature. When I came back to my village I wrote a poem titled "A Poem Sent to Shanghang Town" and send it to him:

> Have the dew drops remained on the grass or disappeared?
> Does the small pavilion at the riverbank
> still remember our dreams and yearnings?

It was published in issue No. 1 of *Fujian Wenyi (Fujian Literature and Art)*, 1980.

My friend, perhaps the lights of the fishing boats have already drifted far away, and perhaps the rock we sat on under an old

---

*Franz Mehring, *Karl Marx: Geschichts seines Leben* (1918).

**The notes included passages from a much broader range of works than were otherwise available during the "cultural revolution".

banyan tree is already covered with a deep Autumn frost, but what you said I never forget: "A work without genuine personal beliefs will never be great literature."

"A Poem Sent to Shanghang Town" was the first poem I published, but it was far from being the first one I had written. Many young friends ask me how I began writing, and what I've told you might seem a superfluous answer. But it's very possible that I would not have written poems if I had not had friendships (my heart still seeks friends as a sunflower sees sunlight), or if I had not had the bittersweet experiences of life in a mountain village, or my teachers' perceptive suggestions about my writing, or the basic knowledge they taught me on many subjects, from history to art, or the influence of Maupassant and Mallarm, or my grandfather teaching me poems when I was so young.

Spreading out,
it is the blood in the loser's heart;
standing up,
it is the monument of the winner.*

Any success, even a small one, is the product of great effort and long-repeated practice.

In 1972 I was allowed to return to the city as an only child, but I was not assigned a job, and I felt stranded. Many years later I was able to understand that being "stranded" was its own kind of life. I often walked up and down the cold, lonely beach:

How lonely is my shadow,
from the beach to the dangerous cliff;
How proud is my heart,
from sunset to the silence of night.**

---

* " Pearl: A Tear of the Ocean, "*A Boat with Two Masts*, p. 8.
** "To the Great Sea" (1973).

I was not accepted by society or understood by the people around me. I suffered from degradation and felt as though I were living in an icy cellar. But the "joy of coming back to life"* was silently flowing, like the green sap of Spring in the branches and buds.

What was it that was coming back to life? It was a consciousness that questioned and challenged the established ideology and that sought to restore the true face of life. "Don't tell us what we should do, let us think why and what we want to do. Let us make our own choices and be able to feel our personal responsibility to history and to our nation.

In 1973 I was assigned to a series of temporary jobs at a construction company, as a propaganda writer, statistician, furnace operator, guide, and bricklayer. I willingly put aside any trace of my intellectualism. I listened to the old workers telling about their difficult lives, and I joined in the jokes of the boorish young workers. I streamed with sweat as I shovelled. I felt the vibration of the factory where we produced pre-fabricated concrete buildings. On night shifts I often went with a group that stole sweet potatoes from a nearby field and then boiled them for supper in an iron pot. Those potatoes tasted very salty because the field had such poor, alkaline soil. But I was happy because my companions forgot that I wore glasses and that I had books hidden in my pack. Because of my solidarity with the workers they didn't care if I read *Aesthetic Criticism of Matthew Arnold* during the hour of rest time in a smelly shed, stretched out on cement bags, with my head resting on a brick.

I always think of myself as one of the ordinary laborers. My sadness and happiness are all from this land soaked with sweat and tears. Motherland, I belong to you, even though I am only a reed and perhaps you have more valuable white birches and azaleas.

I only wrote poetry occasionally, sometimes to add to a letter

---

*Ibid.

and sometimes just casually on a scrap of paper. I passed them to friends who shared my interest in poetry. Many of those poems are now lost. Some people might criticize me for not writing about smelting furnaces and scaffolding, but I had tried that earlier and the poems were very bad. One day I chanced to see an older worker, to whom I was an apprentice, outside the low wall of a temple. He was secretly using old-fashioned divining for help about his son's unemployment. I and the mountains and the jequirty bean vines watched him in silence and sympathy. I only listened and thought again and again, standing there in the misty rain at dusk. I did not recite poems to him about "doing away with superstitions." Instead I preferred to tell him stories during breaks at work, using my own words and choosing an appropriate story like *The House of the Seven Gables* or *Les Miserables*.* I was not so naive as to think that my poems could ever reach a harbor in those hearts.

There are many ways besides poetry to reach another heart. A person who has a sense of what is right and who is sympathetic eventually will find some way, not just poetry, to communicate to the world. Hope and despair, smiles and bitterness, all can be expressed by poetry, but none of them can only be expressed by poetry.

In 1975, because of my poems that were circulated among friends, I became acquainted with an older poet from my native Fujian.** Ever since then we have been good friends. I respect and trust him for the truth and tireless zeal of his artistic pursuits, and also for his steadfast view of life, which has retained traces of childlike innocence. I kept up our friendship even dur-

---

*Nathaniel Hawthorne, *The House of the Seven Gables* (1851); Victor Hugo, *Les Miserables* (1862).

**This refers to Cai Qijiao (b. 1918), a poet and teacher. He studied literature in Yan'an at the Lu Xun Academy of Arts and won prizes for poetry in 1941. He was attacked during the 1950s for not paying sufficient regard to ideology in his writing. During the early 1970s he was sent to reform as a laborer in Yongan, Fujian. He began publishing poems again in the late 1970s.

ing his political difficulties, when everyone else was turning a cold shoulder towards him and his friends. He generously copied out and sent to me many poems and essays about poetry. He practically forced me to read translations of poems by Neruda and Baudelaire, and introduced me to many modern foreign poets. I still have some of those letters in which he copied out long paragraphs from critical essays and added his own comments. I was especially moved by his own poems. I acknowledge that I have been deeply influenced by him in many ways.

During those days, many of the "teachers" were ones who would think that $1/2 + 1/3 = 1/5$. But my efforts to find a teaching job were unsuccessful, even at the schools run by local people. Once again I was faced with an impassable chasm between one's dream and reality:

> The limitless sea,
> whose horizon is always beyond distance,
> in that several meters
> loses its power*.

My friend the old poet quickly sent his answer in a poem: "Suffering,/ should turn into ears of sympathy for others!" I still keep that two line poem under the glass top of my desk.

Before this I had only a vague yearning to contribute to society, to pursue truth, and to show concern for human life. "Suffering, / should turn into tears of sympathy for others!" Those lines gave me a clear direction. I instinctively knew that crying for others is not enough; a helping hand is nec-

---

*Lines 5-8 of the second stanza of "Sailboat" (1975), *A Boat with Two Masts*; that stanza begins:
> The Sea's surf at flood tide
> is only a few meters from this boat,
> the waves seething,
> the seabirds flapping overhead watchfully.

essary: "If you are the fire, / I am willing to be the coal."*
When you cheer up and begin to help others you will gain focus and support.

That was the underlying premise for the poems I wrote in 1975, when I worked in a textile mill. In 1977 I became a solderer in a light bulb factory. I have never had much physical strength, but my jobs required quite heavy work. My daily trip to the factory took a half hour longer than most other people's because I had to ride the ferry across the Wujing River. I suffered for sometimes hating that beautiful, gentle river for lengthening my journey. When I was on the long night shift I thought the stars were as pale and feeble as sleepless eyes, and in the early morning mist the street lights looked like spinning balls. Some people who read my poems imagined that I lived amidst comfort and beauty, and one of them wrote to me in 1976, "The morning flowers and evening moon in Gulangyu nurture your exquisitely wrought heart." I wrote back, "I don't know there are morning flowers and an evening moon because I have seen only storms these past years."

When I wrote "Motherland, My Dear Motherland,"** I had just started on the night shift and I wanted very much to go outside for a walk under the starlit sky with the wind cooling my burning cheeks. But I couldn't leave the assembly line. Often when those thoughts made me inattentive to my work, drops of hot solder would fall on my fingers, raising lots of blisters. One editor criticized my poem "The Assembly Line"*** as "low-spirited, obscure and not conforming to the life of young female workers." He must have thought that only descriptions like "the silver shuttle is dancing" fit the feelings of "young female workers." I still wonder today who can really tell the feelings of young female workers.

---

* "For You" (1975).
** Written April 20, 1979.
*** "The Assembly Dine" (January-FEbruary 1980), *A Boat with Two Masts*.

When I close my eyes I can recall the days when I was a young female worker: On weekend evenings I would hurriedly change from my work clothes, wring out my wet hair, and go to the shore with friends. We liked to sit on rock that was uncovered only at low tide. The wind was joyously wild and the lights were confusing. We almost felt we could fly away. But the illusion could not replace real life. And since we couldn't escape real life, we should seize it. The "beautiful sorrow" of my early years was replaced by serious thoughts, and I wrote "The Assembly Line."

That poem has been continually attacked, even by the critics who otherwise like it, for what they call its "limitation" of "not calling forth people's passion to change the reality." Our literary critics seem to think that no matter how great a writer is, he must have limitations. Their judgments follow the pattern that the writer hasn't found the power of the proletariat class or hasn't found the road to revolution, etc. But a gifted writer is neither a judge nor a wizard, and artistic works are not magical potions. Tolstoy said that an artist's purpose is not to offer logical solutions to problems, but to make people love life by revealing its inexhaustible phenomena.

I have never considered myself a true poet. I just write poems for others. Even though I believe that literature must express genuine personal beliefs, I also know that I will never be a thinker, at least not while I am writing a poem. I would rather be led by my feelings and not put my trust in the mathematical way of thinking. In 1977, when I first read Bei Dao's poems, it was like the shock of a powerful earthquake. I felt like a cassia tree struggling to grow in a small yard, and then finding a hyacinth seed from afar which allows the tree to comprehend the boundless world by imagining lawns and oases. I like his poems very much and I was overjoyed to discover "This is All," which led me to write the poem "This Is Also 'All'":

not all seeds
fail to find some soil to root in;*

In our sensitive land no matter how weak a sincere voice may be it will cause an enduring echo.

I do not want to analyze Bei Dao's poetry here, nor the poems of Jiang He, Mang Ke, Gu Cheng, or Yang Lian, because I am not able to do that very well. However, their influence on me has been profound. After reading their poems, I did not dare to write at all during 1978 and 1979. I still don't think of them as a "modernist" school. Each has his own style, and at the same time they share a spirit of exploration. As I understand, they and all of the youths of my generation who have the high aspirations self-consciously tie their destiny to that of our nation. I was moved by their hard work and their spirit of self-sacrifice.

The terminology that literary critics use today to describe those poems and mine, such as "not understandable," "misty," or "obscure" are just temporary. Mankind's advance towards a more sophisticated civilization will not be a glorious parade in which, when the officer orders "column left," the inner file will march in small steps and the outer files will march in increasingly larger steps so that the whole army advances in perfectly executed, fan-shaped ranks. The forerunners are always solitary, and they often remain anonymous:

Still, they will have left their conflicting tracks
for those who follow after,
and signed besides the necessary papers for their entry.**

A gold-colored beetle is calling for help on my window. I open the windows and door and watch it fly slowly toward the blossoming cassia tree. I wish that every longing for freedom will have someone pay attention to it.

---

*Written July 25, 1977.
** "To My Generation" (1980).

Complete Silence from the Clarity Gained through Sadness

IN early November 1981 the rich beauty of Autumn would soon wither away. The fragrance of snow-white cordate tuberose still clung to the branches. I put a sixteen-section poem, "The Singing Iris," into an envelope and put the top on my pen. I thought that I would stop writing for a while, but I could not have imagined that it would be for three years.

As the quiet dusk embraced me, before I knew it my excited mood became peaceful. Moments like that always bring memories of my mother, for when I was little, the dusk was the only time of the day I could share with her. I would set my little bamboo chair close to her while she played a zither. Her fingers were white butterflies on the quivering strings. The sad "Song of the Black Horse" floated into the dream-like twilight and touched the heart. I watched her with utmost concentration. My heart wanted to absorb, bit by bit, all of her beauty, so fresh after her bath. Several years later, when I was sent off to a mountain village, I was crossing a bridge in the moonlight and suddenly heard a familiar tune, as the faint but sonorous notes of a guitar were carried to me by the evening air. The sounds seemed to be waiting everywhere for me to capture. Tears came to my eyes and a confusion of feelings welled up on my heart. The sounds of the guitar must have come from the heavens.

Mama's rich emotions but weak disposition did her great harm. She was unable to adapt herself to the ruthless political denouncements and she died filled with bitterness. I have inherited part of my mother's disposition. (When she was only ten years old she sat at the door crying for not being able to sleep; I remember at age eleven or twelve getting out of bed at midnight to secretly take mama's sleeping pills.) I have passed this disposition on to my two-year-old son. When someone pretends to scare children, or even raises his fist at a picture of a car or a cat, my son will scream in protest and burst into tears.

Sensitivity and opposition to violence are good parts of the human heart, but kindheartedness can bring suffering to one's life. There are many causes of suffering, but each can be a poison. Unless one has the sunlight of idealism as a guide and unless one heeds "an irresistible call"* how else can one have strength to overcome the endless obstacles in his path?

When I was young I tried many foolish ways to cure myself of crying too easily, to overcome my fear of the dark, and to correct my arrogant aloofness. When I was in the countryside I met a cadre who had been sent there to be an ordinary laborer. He told me he could work for three days without eating, that he could eat more than a pound of rice at one meal, that he could have sweet dreams even if he slept standing up, squatting, or lying uncomfortably on a shoulder pole. I absolutely worshipped him and tried to do some similar things. One cold day I wore a thin blouse and went down to the stream, where I drank a lot of its icy water. Unfortunately, that night I had a high fever and fell into unconscious. My fellows were very frightened and went all around the village searching for medicine for me. But today I can only sigh over all my failed efforts to strengthen my physical constitution, which has never improved. I was very fond of Jack London's *The Sea-Wolf* and *White Fang** and also Hemingway's novels. I copied down in my notebook quotations from those incomparable adventurers. I never became tough, but my mother's misfortune taught me a lesson, and so I adopted a resilient attitude toward life — my tough old grandma told me a folk saying, "Roll up your trouser legs," which helped me get through those muddy days.

---

* "Perhaps — To an author in isolation" (December 1979), *A Boat with Two Masts*.

**These two novels by Jack London were published in 1904 and 1906.

I am worried about my son, but I know I must let him learn things for himself. My devoted love can be a blue sky over his cradle, but cannot be an umbrella to protect him when he goes through the wide world. My son, you will also have suffering. Please remember: "Idealism makes suffering glorious."*

In that Autumn dusk in 1981 I faced a turning point in my life. I hoped that the sky would always be blue, I believed I could "run laughing through the street"** with my generation, and that we would never again have to nervously skirt the big-character poster wall. I thought the wings of illusion could fly freely from foreign Christmas trees and the Leaning Tower of Pisa to the aeolian bell of Liuhe Pagoda, and from the ancient magical flute to modern ice skates. At least our wish to understand wondrous beauty would no longer be attacked as "feudalism, capitalism, and revisionism." But why I have forgotten that I just wrote:

Ah, the wandering shadow.
do you stretch out your tentacles again?***

Was the shadow waiting for its chance to absorb me? Only me? "The Singing Iris" was not the first sting I felt. In 1980 the provincial magazines debated the New Poetry, and used my poems as examples. My name was like a worn-out ball being kicked back and forth between the two sides. The crowd didn't just applaud or hiss, some of them threw rotten fruit and eggs. On the first day of the Spring Festival I cried all day because of those unexpected, harsh slanders. An old friend sat with me at the shore until midnight. The sea whispered as its waves gently rose and fell. I remarked how peaceful and easy it must be beneath its surface of the sea. I thank my friend, who was just an ordinary worker, for giving me a reply that was apt and very

---
*From her poem "The Singing Iris" (1981).
** "The Singing Iris."
*** "The Montage of Dusk" (1981).

convincing: "It may be so, but it's also lonely and ice cold."

I no longer cry so easily at those rumors. I have been forced to realize that my idealism is my only "god," and that it decides everything. As the Bible says: "You should carry the cross on your back every day. Follow me."*

In 1982 I kept silent because a restless little life inside me took all my attention. I had a long stay in the hospital because of difficulties with my pregnancy. Every day in the hospital I read articles from one place after another about "The Singing Iris." The poem was singing among its readers. It was like a clever pet "eight-note" bird that sings particularly well when it's under good care, but will wither away if it's treated viciously. I was more surprised than angry that the poem would bring so much trouble, and even personal attacks on me. But I did not explain myself at that time, and I won't now or in the future. A line from the Bible says: "We will all stand in front of God someday."** I might mention, by the way, that I grew up in a Christian family but I don't believe in a god.

Many kind readers sent their regards. The lush Spring grass grew outside my window. Enthusiastic editors sent letters offering to publish *A Boat with Three Masts* or *A Boat with Four Masts*, referring to my future books. Correspondence study colleges invited me to join their editorial boards or be a consultant. Many admiring eyes gathered around me. Magazines even asked to have my smile on their covers, so my smile could become part of the scenery in the poetry garden. Newspaper reporters offered to help me refute the rumors about me; they wanted to use my tears to call for redress of the troubles of all Chinese women writers. The local and national television stations asked me to appear on their programs to use my voice and my eyes to put right the worries of my admirers.

---

*Luke 9:23.
**Romans 14:10.

But I refused all of those.
I rather keep silent.

My true friends, with such warm hearts, please forgive me. When you received only brief replies to your letters you may have thought that my silence was a sign of my lack of literary skill. When you endured the hardship of a long journey to visit me and then I refused to see you, or when I rejected your invitations (for even the most tactfully worded rejection is a disappointment), you may have thought me arrogant and eccentric. If you have seen me knitting sweaters for my mother-in-law and my son you may have thought that my silence was caused by despondency. I hope you won't believe that my silence was from cowardice and that I was hiding in a bunker because I was frightened by the turmoil afflicting literary circles during the past three years, and that I watched with indifference — as one might watch fires on the other side of a river. You should know that in our closely bound society all fires will eventually cross the river.

Being silent behind words
is worth it.

Yes, "Being silent behind words . . . being silent so, and not betraying" requires drawing "on lifelong courage and honesty."* Sometimes one needs to risk his life in the pursuit of truth and art; even pursuing just the right to having a normal life and love requires courage. Sometimes one needs courage to remain unsullied, to despise authority, to be honest regardless of praise and honor or blame and disgrace, and to be willing to endure loneliness.

I also recall my father, who experienced so much hardship in his life. After my mother died he took care of all the housework, cooking, washing clothes, and sewing quilts, so his skinny daughter could have time to read "sage's books," even when

---

*"The Heart Has Its Own Law" (1976).

she worked on the night shift. After the Tiananmen Incident in 1976, the news of searches for anti-revolutionary poems bore down menacingly, and father finally begged me, "Please burn all your poems." He watched my face and added, with fear and anxiety, "I speak from experience."

"Don't you still have my brother and sister? Just think of me as already dead."

Father dejectedly lowered his head and walked away, sighing, "If you get into political trouble do you think your brother and sister and I will have any peace? You don't understand...."

How could I not understand? Father, that afternoon I stood in the small garden you had made with bricks and mud, bit by bit. The canna blossoms are so lovely they don't seem to notice the heavy clouds and rain outside the bamboo fence. Yes, father, you pulled the coal cart and carried heavy packages on your shoulder, you saved five cents from breakfast to buy flower seeds, you were a banker moving the beads of an abacus as gracefully as if you were playing the strings of a zither. But don't you still need a small piece of land, covered with green leaves and plentiful flowers, where you can preserve your deep feelings, your faded dreams of youth, your grief, your loneliness, and your comfort?

Recently I received a letter from a reader who gave no salutation and no signature. The letter's only contents are a handwritten copy of my poem "The Heart Has Its Own Law." I understand you, dear friend; you ask me to keep to my word:

> the strongest protest
> and the most courageous honesty
> are not greater than — living
> and then speaking out.*

I planned to write out the conversation with my father in my reply and to tell that reader: When the threat of a sword hangs over my head, any carelessness may bring disaster. There are

---

* The closing lines of that poem.

still countless numbers of people like rows of small trees unwillingly bent but indomitably spreading their life-sustaining roots, building to a surge from deep in the earth. They look for sources of truth and they store the energy of sunlight so they can finally offer their hearts as fruit to the slowly arriving season. Today, in the early 1980s, the great wave of social reform not only renews economic life, it will dredge out many silted-up channels of spiritual rivers. Even though there are still a few injurious darts flying, the years of "Dying, for a flower" and "Being silent behind words"* will never again turn its grimacing face to terrify us.

Everybody knows that our nation did not reach today's openness by an easy parade with marching music, along a wide, straight street, with the crowds on each side waving flowers dreamily. The crowds and the people walking in the street all have their own painful experiences and are sharp-eyed. They can understand: sometimes being silent can be effective speech.

I think that at each important change or turning point in a person's life he comes to a new stage of feeling and experience. For an artist or writer, his work, which usually expresses his feeling and experience, also reaches a fork in the road. At that moment a person's silence can be an indication that he is gathering strength while pondering the choice of a new direction. My silence is also due, at least to some small extent, by my having grown up in a broken family. My parents loved us more than do most parents, and my grandma's rough hands were full of warmth. My mother never cried in front of us, but in the morning I would find tear stains beside my pillow in our shared bed. Until I was in the fifth grade I did not know that the man who sometimes waited for me at the end of our alley holding a gift of eggs was my father.

---

* " The Heart Has Its Own Law."

At the beginning of the "cultural revolution" my mother realized it was futile to try to protect her children's future from the influence of their father's Rightist political shadow. So she agreed to a reconciliation with my father. He was as happy as if he had found treasures. He has kept us from economic difficulty since then, even when we were sent to the countryside. But the years of depression about the family's situation made my mother sick.... I will never let my son carry memories as heavy as those in my heart.

What I want most is to be a virtuous wife and a good mother.

People have reminded me that I do not belong only to my son, and have advised me to be more a part of our era. Yes, my son belongs not only to me but to the future of our country. I say that not as a political cliche. (When our sensitive ears reject political cliches, we should be careful not to reject the truth that can be in those cliches.) I sympathize deeply with successful career women when their tender hearts are hurt by the unfamiliar cries of their children. Even though I revere those women's devotion to their careers, I can't imitate them. I'm just a normal woman in my emotions and in my livelihood. I never intended to be a writer or poet. Even the lightest laurel would be too heavy for my simplicity. I don't want to be an object on display like a potted plant or a rare bird. I don't want to "be the stone star of a famous cliff a thousand years."*

However, if it were necessary for me to leave my son [because of duty to my motherland], I would have the courage to say:

> I leave a vacant position
> On the flood control dam,
> Let all the waves that had clashed me
> also lash at you.
> I have no regret.
> You should not avoid them.

---

* "Goddess Peak" (June 1981).

In his novel *Jean-Christophe*, Romain Rolland writes that when a person is young he should have a dream and feel that he is participating in the great events of history and that his senses correspond with the breath of the universe.* It's a common saying that everyone is a poet when he is young. In the old times, when poets got drunk and discussed literature they would do things that were so shocking that the "neighbor's wall fell down" and "overturned the foreign bed" because their heads were so turned by their talent.** Why can't we be magnanimous toward youth's great ambitions? They might as well be wildly arrogant and outrageous. Each generation's youth has it own different form of expression that responds to the social background. My wildest arrogant action was to lie on a damp wooden bed, looking up at the leaking roof in the countryside, and read my poems to my roommate. I argued in favor of my poems by invoking the names of great foreign poets. My sighs would express radical thinking: It would be a great sorrow if young people didn't have the chance to be wildly arrogant.

People often ask me: "Which of your poems is your favorite?" I steal a remark from the king of soccer, Pele, "My best shot is the next one."

I haven't tried to make a shot during the past three years, but from ones passed to me by the young new players (they send me so many poems in handwritten or mimeographed copies or from local magazines), I see clearly that the best shots, using the best angles, showing the greatest skill, and achieving a goal, are by those youths.

Let us applaud them and toss out hats in celebration. Several

---

*Romain Rolland (1866-1944), *Jean-Christophe* (10 vols, 1904-12); the reference could be to Vol. 3, *Youth*, near the end of Part I, "The House of Euler" or the Vol. 5, *The Market-Place*, near the start of Part III.

**Liu Kezhuang (1187-1269), *ci* to the tune of "A Spring of Plum Blossoms," *Song Ci Xuan* [collection of *ci*-poetry of the Song dynasty], Beijing: Zhonghua shuju, 1962.

years ago, a poet of an older generation showed a sensibly lenient attitude toward his young competitors: "They should be better than us. If not, what kind of future can we expect?"

Let's turn back to this beautiful Autumn day in November 1984. People haven't forgotten me during the past three years, even though I was silent. I often received old or new guests, and I answered five or six thousand letters from readers. Many editors continued to send their magazines to me, regardless of the stormy criticism. What they sent me was really their deep love and warmth. I am sincerely grateful to the editors of *Modern Literature and Art Exploration* magazine for asking me to write this essay. I originally planned to write only "Thank You" and have it printed in a small corner of their magazine. Unexpectedly, my eyes moistened with tears. When did I say "I no longer cry so easily"?

Let me start the epilogue of the poem I wrote three years ago:

> Just come to see me,
> Come in the morning,
> You will find me
> in people's love,
> and find your
> singing iris.*

November 24, 1984

---

* "The Singing Iris."

图书在版编目(CIP)数据

心烟——舒婷诗文选：英文/舒婷著；吴德安等译—北京：中国文学出版社，1995.4

ISBN 7-5071-0285-8

I.心... II.①舒...②吴... III.①诗歌-作品集-中国-当代-英文 ②散文-作品集-中国-当代-英文 IV.I227

心烟 —— 舒婷诗文选

熊猫丛书
*
中国文学出版社出版
(中国北京百万庄路24号)
中国国际图书贸易总公司发行
(中国北京车公庄西路35号)
北京邮政信箱第399号　邮政编码100044
1995年　第1版（英）
ISBN 7-5071-0285-8
0 1200
10-E-2984P